THE ULTIMATE GUIDE TO SELLING YOUR HOME

JUNE'S TEAM SECRETS TO ATTRACT TOP-DOLLAR OFFERS ON YOUR PROPERTY

This guide includes helpful information about our team, tips, checklists, and research that will guide you through the exciting process of selling your home. Refer to this guide early and often during your home-selling journey. Don't be afraid to reach out and ask questions about the guide or the home-selling process. We are here for you every step of the way!

Thank you for the opportunity to present our qualifications and marketing plan for selling your property. The journey of selling a home is filled with significant decisions, memories, and emotions. Understanding this, I am truly honored that you are considering entrusting this important chapter to June's Team.

Selecting the right realtor is paramount. It's not just about placing a sign in your yard and listing your property online; it's about a partnership built on trust, knowledge, and a shared vision. We recognize the immense responsibility that comes with representing your home and your interests.

This guide has been crafted with diligence and care, mirroring the very ethos we bring to each transaction. Within these pages, you will discover the secrets and strategies that have made June's Team a trusted name in real estate in the Northern Colorado community. Our commitment is not merely to sell your home, but to secure its value, to tell its story, and to attract offers that reflect its true worth.

As you leaf through "The Ultimate Guide to Selling Your Home," know that our team stands ready to transform these words into action, and most importantly, results. I and my team look forward to meeting with you and helping you through this process. We are prepared to answer any and all of your questions and walk with you each step of the way.

Warmest regards,

June Lemmings

970-388-3692 Cell
970-573-5791 Office
www.junelemmings.com
june@junesteam.com

Table of Contents

06   June's Story
08   Customer Satisfaction - Testimonials
10   Our Process
14   Why June's Team
16   Meet Our Team
19   Building the Foundation
35   Time to Sell
39   Marketing
44   Showing Your Home
49   Closing
57   Frequently Asked Questions

June's STORY

In 2002 I moved back to Northern Colorado after going through a divorce because I wanted to be back with my family. I was living in Oklahoma City at the time and in management at a large call center that was cutting-edge in technology, a division of AOL. I managed 60 people there and was succeeding in my role. When things changed for me personally and I went through a divorce, I suddenly became a single mother of two. Within four days of being back, I saw an ad in the newspaper that asked, "Why rent when you can own?" I actually called the person listed. He was a real estate investor, and I ended up going to work for him. 1 1/2 years later, I got my real estate license. I feel fortunate that my start in the field was learning about real estate as an investment opportunity; seeing the world through investors' eyes helped me open my eyes to a new facet of this industry. I see the value of homeownership from resale to rentals and truly look at real estate as an investment.

With that baseline of experience, I began to learn the emotional aspects of the field by working with buyers and sellers. In college, I studied Psychology, and I believe this area of study has proven beneficial in my work as a REALTOR®. I am like a counselor in some ways. I walk people through emotions and reactions when it comes to buying or selling their home. I describe my work as similar to a pilot. I tell my clients that there could be some turbulence, but my job is to land them safely. There are things that may come up suddenly, but by being solution-oriented and proactive, I can typically diffuse these quickly.

I have a deep understanding of working through challenges and I am truly passionate about helping homeowners and helping the process be as seamless as possible.

I worked during college for MCI Long Distance and became the number two agent in the United States. I paid most of my way through college at AIMS and at UNC by working three jobs and also receiving a President's Scholarship and others. I had high grades and a strong work ethic. It is this background that fuels me. I am an ongoing pursuer of education. I love to learn. I also believe if you want to achieve something, you really can do it.

Supporting small companies and other women in business, along with charities, are cornerstones of how I operate. I am an active participant in the Northern Colorado Women in Business networking group. I am also very active in the community and I volunteer for Habitat for Humanity, Zac's Legacy, and 60-plus Rides, plus many more. I contribute to the Food Bank of Weld County and am a Gold Spur Sponsor of the Greeley Stampede. I believe in giving back to the community and that it's just good business. I want to work hard and volunteer so I can support the community that supports me.

My number one goal in my business is to create "raving fans." I read a book by that name, and it taught me so much about taking service to the next level. I believe in investing a lot of extra money in marketing for my sellers, in particular, and doing things that go beyond their expectations. Having an assistant and team members who can answer questions when I am at showings is a plus for my clients and has helped save time in the buying and selling process.

I am an empire builder and I want to keep expanding, to keep on top of the latest technology, and help others grow so they can have successful careers. My goal is to create relationships for life with my clients, which has helped me to be a stand-out in the industry. I love to throw client appreciation parties to show my gratitude. In the end, I want everyone who works with me to feel important and recognized and know that I am looking out for their best interests. This is my goal and what will keep my business growing and successful and my clients happy.

Motto:
Treat others the way you want to be treated.

CLIENT SATISFACTION

Our clients are at the heart of everything we do, and we have the testimonials to prove it!

"I am so glad we decided to sell with June's Team. I live in Greeley, Colorado and June Lemmings was a great realtor and her transaction coordinator Colleen was amazing. June gave us a fair price point to sell our house, and it sold in fewer days than she told me to expect. She had several open houses for us and did a virtual tour as well. Anytime I asked for an update on a viewing she was quick to find out what the viewers thought and respond back to me. This was our third house to sell, and she was easily the best realtor I've worked with." -Amanda W.

"June has been a professional, kind, resourceful agent helping my spouse and I sell our home and getting us into a home and city we love! She listens and understands our wants and needs while so very helpful with all of the hurdles involved with home selling and buying. Her team has got you covered as well!" -Robbie R.

"June and the team were absolutely wonderful to work with while selling my home. Even during a pandemic, the team was responsive and on top of things! The photographer June set up did a wonderful job portraying my home and we sold it very quickly! 10/10 would recommend!" -Cindy H.

"June and her team are amazing. We expressed to her what we needed with the sale if our home and June was able to make it happen for us! As an older couple not having sold a home in 20 years, we had no idea of the process in today's housing market. June walked us through it every step of the way and even got us help to prepare the house for showing! Her team is kind, helpful, and very understanding. The whole team made this process as easy and stress-free as possible. We would highly recommend June's Team with Keller Williams to anyone looking to sell their home! 5 Stars and more!" -Theresa H.

"I have never had a realtor be so prompt and responsive in the past. As soon as I spoke to June, she was ready to come over to see the place, go over the realtor contact, walk me through the things to come, and suggest what I could sell my home for. She, and her whole team, took such good care of me. I received timely check-ins and updates, they brought box labels and boxes when I needed them.. they even went the extra mile and brought us a pie for Thanksgiving... I don't know of any other realtor that has cared so much for their clients. I highly recommend June and her team when you're in the market. An absolute pleasure working with her, a flawless transaction, and in record time from start to closing." -Irish C.

"June is top-notch!!! She helped us get a great deal on our new home AND got us top dollar on our home!! We are so pleased we chose the right realtor!!" -Donna S.

"June and her team are exceptional! We used her in purchasing our first home and now again for our dream home as a family of four! Her team is kind, professional, and makes the home buying process easy and fun!" -Deanna B.

"I first met June when I was looking for a home to purchase in Greeley. It was evening and I still had a trip back to Parker to make. A listing popped up just as I was leaving. I took a chance and called her. She said someone would meet me there in a few minutes and was waiting when I got there! From the minute I met her and her assistants I knew I had found the right person/agency to help me. She not only is the best agent I have ever used, she is also very committed to the town and the people who live here. Her assistants are great to work with as well. I asked her for a painter and immediately had a phone number. I needed a local mover and she gave me the name of one who specialized in working with Handicapped clients! Her awards are many and well deserved....including multiple honors as Realtor of the Year." -Gail B.

"If you need a realtor in the Greeley area I highly recommend June's Team! June and her team are absolutely wonderful to work with and will find your dream home and sell your old house with ease and get the most value for your home!" -Audra K

"June has been so helpful! She is very dedicated and passionate. June's team has also been very helpful! They are all very welcoming and really want to help their clients find their dream home! We went through hell trying to sell our home with other realtors for over a year and a half and when we met June she made it happen within 3 days of being on the market! She is now assisting us with buying a new home and has been so helpful through the whole process. She's not just our realtor but she is now a friend! We could not have done any of this without her and her team thank you all! June is very trustworthy and loves what she does! There is no better realtor than her!" -Lex M.

"We are in the process of selling our Townhome in Greeley and I have to share the professionalism of June's Team at Keller Williams 1st Realty Associates. This is a 10+ Star Team. The communication, the effort with Open House events and their comprehensive Marketing campaign has been beyond our expectations. They keep us updated every couple of days and we are so pleased to have made the change to have them represent our property. (Yes we had it listed with another firm and making the change was the best decision we made) If anyone is looking to buy or sell, I would urge everyone to put June's Team on your Team. You will be as impressed as we have been. First Class Operation!!" -Brad T

"June is great to work with. She is a great negotiator and takes the time to develop long lasting relationships with her clients." -Andrew E.

Our PROCESS

1 MARKETING CONSULTATION

We will meet with you and talk about all the ways we are going to market your home. A professional photographer will come to your home and take pictures and our team will turn them into a listing. We will use professional pictures and videos for social media posting as well. We will post on social media when your home is considered "coming soon".

2 ON THE MARKET

After your marketing consultation, your listing will be published on multiple listing sites, as well as the other various websites we market to. Your home will have it's own landing page on our website as well.

3 OFFER

Every offer presented will be discussed in detail with you. We will point out the pros and cons of each offer, negotiate with the buyer's agent on your behalf, and earn you the most money in the shortest amount of time. You will always be the one to make the final decision when accepting an offer.

4 NEGOTIATIONS

We will advocate for you during negotiations and help you get the best terms throughout the process such as offers, inspection, and appraisal issues, as well as any other items that may come up.

5 INSPECTION

The buyer's agent and the buyer will attend the inspection. While the inspection is being conducted, you should plan to not be present. General inspections run for about four hours. However, there can be additional inspections such as radon, roof, and sewer scope.

6 REPAIR NEGOTIATIONS

Once the inspection report is received, it will be forwarded to you along with the inspection objection. We will talk through the documents and the buyer's requests together. An agreement will be made that you feel comfortable with for any repairs that will take place.

7 APPRAISAL

An appraiser will come out to your property. The appraiser is hired by a third-party management company and we do not have the option to order our own appraisal, nor does the buyer. They are generally there for less than 30 minutes and will be taking photos, measurements, and making sure the home is in good condition. They also look for health and safety items.

8 CLOSING

Once there is an executed contract on your home, we will schedule the closing with a Title Company and the buyers. We will keep in contact with the Title Company to make sure they have all the documents they need and keep in contact with the buyer's agent and your mortgage professional to make sure everyone receives necessary updates. We will also review the final settlement statement, and verify that the proceeds have been received.

Our
HIGHLIGHTS

WHY KELLER WILLIAMS REALTY

RELIABILITY

Founded on the principles of trust and honesty, Keller Williams Realty emphasizes the importance of having the integrity to do the right thing and always putting your client's needs first. Our belief is that our success is ultimately determined by the legacy we leave with each client we serve.

KELLER WILLIAMS is #1 in the world!

TRACK RECORD

We are proud to work for the world's largest real estate franchise by agent count. It's proof that when you offer a superior level of service, the word spreads fast.

KNOWLEDGE

Keller Williams Realty stands out as the world's largest real estate franchise, and for good reason. Recognized by Training Magazine as the top training company across all sectors, Keller Williams consistently stays ahead of real estate trends through its extensive and forward-thinking curriculum. Being a part of such an esteemed network ensures that our team at June's Team is always equipped with the latest insights and tools, allowing us to provide you with exceptional service at every turn.

WHY JUNE'S TEAM

EXCELLENCE

Throughout my 20+ years working with buyers, sellers, and investors, I've gained the experience and knowledge to understand the unique challenges that can be presented with each client's unique real estate needs. Not only that, I'm highly proficient at understanding the current market and how to work with the fast-paced changes that are inevitable in real estate. I believe in going the extra mile for my clients to help them not only find the perfect home but also to help them transition and thrive successfully in their community.

To become a top performer in the industry, I have jumped through many hoops and overcome multiple hurdles to go to bat for my clients. I am proud to have received many awards for the work I do in the community, but I am even more proud to have clients return to me because of the positive experience they had with me and my team. Serving the residents of Northern Colorado is an honor and my love for the community is continuously growing.

SPECIALTIES

- Certified Negotiation Expert
- Buyer's Agent
- Seller's Agent
- Relocation
- New Construction
- Investment Properties
- Awarded 5-Star Certification in 2023
- Awarded Best of Greeley Real Estate Team 2020, 2021, 2023
- Awarded Best of Greeley Realtor 2022
- Top 100 agents in the Colorado region
- Seniors Real Estate Specialist®
- Certified Distressed Property Expert®
- Certified Residential Specialist
- Certified Military Residential Specialist

In the end, I want everyone who works with me to feel important and recognized and know that I am looking out for their best interests.

Meet OUR TEAM

June Lemmings
Team Lead, Associate Broker, Seller's Agent

- Oversee all Transactions
- Expert Negotiator
- Senior Real Estate Specialist
- Team Coordination
- Community Connections
- Real Estate Wealth Strategist
- Certified Residential Specialist
- Staging Certification

Jennifer Peterson
Transaction Coordinator

- Contract to Close
- Assisting Clients
- Guaranteeing a smooth transaction process

Lane Lemmings
Seller Concierge

- Photography/Vidiography/Drone
- Listing Assistance
- Assisting Sellers

Meet OUR TEAM

Gered Stovall
Licensed Buyer's Specialist

- Showings
- Open Houses
- Research & Follow-up

Itza Salazar
Licensed Buyer's Specialist / Bilingual

- Showings
- Open Houses
- Research & Follow-up

Julie Leafgren
Licensed Buyer's Specialist

- Showings
- Open Houses
- Research & Follow-up

Kyra Andersen
Team Support

- Client Event Planning
- Assisting with Client Care
- Help with Marketing for Sellers

With full service, we offer your choice of 4 hours handyman service, house cleaning, painting or help with packing.

Pre-Market
BUILDING THE FOUNDATION FOR SELLING YOUR HOME

You have made the decision to sell your home and you want to sell it for top dollar. Now what? There are some important factors that every homeowner should consider at this stage. We will walk you through each consideration in more detail.

Determining THE BEST TIME TO SELL

- Understand Market Trends: Identify if it's a buyer's or seller's market.

- Check Your Finances: Make sure selling is financially viable, considering equity, mortgage status, and any prepayment penalties.

- Life Changes: Relocation, family size changes, or lifestyle shifts can influence the timing.

- Home Condition: Consider if renovations could boost your home's value. A pre-sale inspection from us will identify beneficial repairs.

- Professional Advice: Consult with June's Team for tailored advice and a comparative market analysis.

- Plan Your Move: Have a plan for your next residence, whether purchasing another home or renting. We can also help you relocate as a buyer.

- Legal and Tax Considerations: Be aware of any tax implications from the sale and ensure there are no legal issues with your property.

- List for Maximum Impact: Time your listing for when it will gain the most visibility. We will help you determine when this is best for your property.

- Emotional Preparedness: Selling a home is a big step. Make sure you're ready for the change.

How do I know if the market is balanced?

If no new homes were listed for sale, it would take about six months to sell all the homes on the market.

Market Conditions

UNDERSTANDING REAL ESTATE MARKETS

The first step in your home-selling journey is to understand whether you are facing a buyer's or seller's market, which is determined primarily by the number of homes on the market and their rate of sale. The number of homes available for purchase is a critical element in determining who holds the advantage in the housing market; you as a seller or your potential home buyers. Generally, more than six months of inventory leads to an advantage for the buyer. Less than six months of inventory typically favors the seller. Remember that even locally, markets vary based on price point and location.

In today's market, things can change quickly due to interest rate fluctuations.

Defining your home's MARKET VALUE

Do not be too quick to mentally lock into a price for your home until you know its true value. A comparative market analysis (CMA) can more accurately determine your home's value. A CMA is a complimentary, no-obligation evaluation of the current value of any given property. CMAs are generated by considering:

- Recent Sales Data: Analysis of similar-style homes recently sold in the area to understand current market conditions.
- Home Features and Upgrades: Unique attributes of a home, including renovations, additions, and high-end finishes.
- Location: The desirability of the neighborhood, school district, and proximity to amenities and services.
- Market Trends: How the local real estate market is performing, including supply and demand, pricing trends, and seasonal influences.
- Comparable Property Size and Condition: Square footage, lot size, home condition, and age compared to other properties in the vicinity.
- Current Listings: Active listings that represent the competition and help gauge how the market is moving.
- Pending Sales: Sales that are under contract but not yet closed, indicating the future direction of the market.
- Historical Data: Past market data that can inform predictions about future trends.
- Adjustments for Differences: Calculations made for differences between your home and the comparables to arrive at a fair value.
- Local Expertise: Insights from experienced real estate professionals who understand the nuances of the Northern Colorado market.

HOW DOES A CMA DIFFER FROM AN ONLINE ESTIMATE?

When it comes to understanding the true value of your home, a Comparative Market Analysis (CMA) conducted by a seasoned real estate professional is far superior to the estimates you might find online. While online estimates can provide a quick snapshot based on broad data and algorithms, they often lack local insight and current market nuances. A CMA, on the other hand, is a carefully crafted review that compares your property to similar homes in your specific area, considering factors such as location, condition, upgrades, and the current market demand. This personalized analysis goes beyond mere numbers; it reflects a deep understanding of Northern Colorado's unique market trends and provides a more accurate and tailor-made valuation of your home.

A CMA isn't just data; it's the pulse of our market, tailored to the unique story of your home.

Working with a
REAL ESTATE AGENT

By partnering with us, you're choosing a real estate ally who will guide you through every facet of the sale, from expertly staging your home for maximum appeal to strategizing the pricing and skillfully negotiating the deal. Our comprehensive marketing approach is designed to highlight your home's best features, complete with detailed neighborhood profiles, rich local insights, and professional photography that brings your property's story to life. Rest assured, with our partnership, you'll benefit from transparent, experienced advice every step of the way to ensure a smooth and successful sale.

WHY IS THE REALTOR YOU CHOOSE SO IMPORTANT?

The realtor you choose is your advocate, marketing agent, business manager, transaction coordinator, and local market expert rolled into one. Their quality and professionalism can significantly influence the outcome of your home-selling experience. The right realtor not only influences how smoothly the transaction goes but also the profitability and speed of your sale.

The Critical Role
OF THE REALTOR

1. Advocate for you during the entire home selling process.
2. Take time to uncover your goals, objectives, and concerns.
3. Research homes in the area and prepare a competitive market analysis.
4. Provide comps and suggestions on the asking price.
5. Help with decluttering and staging ideas while advising on home repairs and upgrades.

6. Hire a professional real estate photographer and videographer.
7. Craft a thoughtful, compelling property description.
8. Place your home on the agent-only database (MLS) and thousands of public real estate sites like Zillow and Realtor.com.
9. Market the property by providing signage and using print and digital marketing strategies.
10. Host open houses at your request.
11. Manage and coordinate all showing requests with your schedule.

12. Qualify any potential buyers.
13. Negotiate offers on your behalf with buyer agents.
14. Assist with various financial aspects of the home sale.
15. Provide oversight and follow-up related to property inspections, repairs, and appraisals.
16. Assist with gathering essential property documents.
17. Manage all dates and deadlines related to the contract.
18. Monitor buyer's loan status leading up to closing.
19. Work directly with the title company to ensure the accuracy of all closing procedures.
20. Be present at closing to ensure all your interests are protected.

Preparing your Home
FOR THE MARKET

You have made the decision to sell your home and you want to sell it for top dollar. Now what? There are some important factors that every homeowner should consider at this stage, including determining your timeline, market conditions, defining your home's market value, and working with a Realtor.

Everyone's reason for selling is different, and your motivation for selling can influence both your time and the pace at which you move through the selling process. Whether you are looking to put down roots in a new school district before school starts, relocate out of state, secure the perfect nursery before your new addition arrives, or downsize for less maintenance as you near retirement, your ideal timeline is often the largest factor in deciding when to get started with your sale. Do not forget to keep the style and characteristics of your home in mind when envisioning your timeline; certain features, like a back patio or a fireplace, can bring more value in a particular season.

Selling by SEASON

The timing of your sale significantly influences your experience. In Northern Colorado, the market peaks from March to August, but don't worry—homes sell year-round, each season offering unique benefits depending on your situation.

SPRING & SUMMER

With higher inventory during spring and summer, your home faces more competition.

To stand out:

- Price Competitively: Attract immediate interest with competitive pricing, leading to more showings and potentially multiple offers, which can drive up the final sale price.

- Enhance Curb Appeal: First impressions are key. A well-manicured lawn and vibrant garden can make your home the standout choice.

- Maximize Daylight: Longer days mean more showing opportunities. Be flexible and allow potential buyers to view your home in the best natural light.

- Focus on Maintenance: Ensure all systems, especially cooling, are in top condition for inspections that buyers are keen to conduct during warmer months.

- Utilize Seasonal Marketing: Use photos and open houses to highlight your home's summer-ready outdoor living spaces, which are especially appealing in this season.

Buyers are often more motivated as they aim to settle before the new school year. Highlighting neighborhood schools and community features can be especially effective during this time.

FALL

- Highlight Autumn Aesthetics: Use the natural fall backdrop to your advantage by keeping your yard clean of leaves and adding seasonal decorations like pumpkins or wreaths to enhance curb appeal.

- Emphasize Comfort: Make your home feel like a cozy retreat from the brisk weather with warm lighting and by turning on the fireplace during showings, if you have one.

- Adjust for Daylight Savings: As the days get shorter, ensure your home is well-lit for evening showings with quality exterior and interior lighting.

- Showcase the Indoor Experience: Focus on creating a welcoming environment indoors, where buyers can imagine enjoying the space as the weather cools.

- Market for the Holidays: Without overwhelming the space, subtle nods to the upcoming holiday season can make your home feel festive and inviting.

Seller Insight

Shorter days go hand in hand with colder weather. If you feel as though the temperature has dropped, there's a good chance that your viewers will feel that as well. So stick the heating on for a bit to warm things up.

WINTER

- **Keep Pathways Clear:** Ensure that walkways and driveways are free of snow and ice, showing that the home is well-maintained and accessible year-round. Always make sure to shovel sidewalks and driveways for showings.

- **Show Off Seasonal Features:** If your home has features like an efficient heating system or heated floors, make sure these are highlighted in your listing and during showings.

- **Capitalize on Less Competition:** With fewer homes on the market, yours can capture more attention from serious buyers who are looking to move despite the colder weather.

- **Create a Virtual Experience:** Provide high-quality virtual tours for buyers who may prefer to start their search from the warmth of their current home.

- **Offer a Festive Welcome:** A tasteful display of winter cheer with lights or a wreath can make your home feel inviting, even on the coldest days.

UNDERSTANDING BUYER MINDSET

Buyers looking in the fall and winter are often more serious about making a purchase. They may be relocating for jobs at the start of the new year or looking to buy before the end of the tax year for financial reasons. Tailoring your home's presentation and your marketing strategy to these timeframes and motivations can be highly effective.

By embracing the unique characteristics of the fall and winter seasons, you can make your home stand out and appeal to buyers looking for a warm and welcoming place to call their own.

Remember, the right preparation and strategy make any season the right season to sell.

HOME STAGING

PREPARING FOR SHOWINGS

Homes sell as a result of correct pricing and great presentation. We know what it takes to make a terrific first impression that will get your home sold.

ROOMS TO STAGE

Use staging to highlight the most lived-in rooms of the house. The living room, kitchen, and primary bedroom are where buyers will spend most of their time, so make those impressions count.

BUYER APPEAL

When your home is decluttered and impersonalized, buyers can envision themselves there. Staging means cleaning up and presenting the property at its best. Nearly one-third of all sellers stage their property to position it well. Another benefit of staging is how much better your marketing photos will look. <u>Nine out of ten buyers look for homes online.</u> Photos that showcase your property in the best possible way keep buyers coming through your door.

Staging is a quick and inexpensive technique for getting your property sold more quickly and for more money.

RENOVATIONS AND FAST FIXES

When preparing your home for sale, sometimes all that's needed is a coat of paint. It is important not to over-renovate, as some projects can cost more than you will recoup when you sell. We can help you to determine which updates may make sense for your home and neighborhood. We also offer a choice of 4 hours of handyman service, cleaning, or boxing items when you list your home with us. This way we can help fix some of the major things that will affect the price you sell your home for.

HOME UPGRADES WITH THE HIGHEST ROI

- Minor Kitchen Updates: Simple improvements like modernizing appliances, painting cabinets, and updating countertops can refresh the kitchen significantly.

- Bathroom Refresh: Small changes like new fixtures, fresh grout, and leak repairs can enhance the bathroom's appeal.

- Exterior Enhancements: Boost curb appeal with a new front door, garage door, or a fresh paint job.

- Basic Landscaping: Maintain a neat lawn, trim bushes, and add some colorful flowers for an inviting look.

- Flooring Improvements: Replace old carpets or refinish hardwood floors to rejuvenate your home's interior.

- Energy Efficiency: Highlight energy-efficient windows, insulation, and LED lighting for eco-friendly appeal.

- Fresh Paint: A new coat of neutral paint can make the home look clean and well-maintained.

- Roof Maintenance: Ensure the roof is in good condition to reassure buyers of the home's overall upkeep.

- HVAC System: A reliable heating and cooling system is a key selling point. Have your system cleaned and serviced.

- Space Maximization: Adding livable space by finishing a basement or attic can increase your home's value.

THE ULTIMATE INSIDE-THE-HOME STAGING CHECKLIST

- [ ] Rent a storage unit to keep your home uncluttered and organized.

- [ ] De-clutter to help keep your home ready for a showing at any moment.

- [ ] De-personalize your home by removing family photos, collections, and trinkets.

- [ ] Neutralize with paint to make your home more approachable. Some accent walls may be okay.

- [ ] Clean off countertops and tables. Put away small kitchen appliances, toiletries, and even books on your bedside tables.

- [ ] Rearrange your furniture to be more symmetrical.

- [ ] Replace old and excessively bold linens in bedrooms.

- [ ] Maximize unused rooms by staging them as an office, extra bedroom, or even a nursery.

- [ ] Use lighting to your advantage. Open blinds for natural light during daytime showings, and turn on lights and lamps during evening showings.

- [ ] Keep every room of the house (and the garage) clean. Vacuum, dust, and wipe down all surfaces, including blinds, walls, and windows.

- [ ] Get rid of odors. Open windows to air out the home naturally or use odor-absorbing products. Don't overuse air fresheners as these can make buyers think you're trying to hide smells.

- [ ] During the holidays, add a seasonal touch such as a wreath on the front door, but don't go overboard.

THE ULTIMATE OUTSIDE-THE-HOME STAGING CHECKLIST

- [ ] Check the condition of your roof.
- [ ] Clean out and straighten gutters and downspouts.
- [ ] Wash the exterior.
- [ ] Freshen up the paint job or siding.
- [ ] Wash windows inside and out and make sure there are no streaks.
- [ ] Paint the trim, shutters, and any railings.
- [ ] Patch driveway and walkways.
- [ ] Maintain your lawn regularly and re-sod problem areas, if necessary.
- [ ] Replace old mulch with new covering.
- [ ] Place in-ground LED lights on both sides of the front door walkway.
- [ ] Add plants to the front of the house: in-ground, potted, and window boxes.
- [ ] Get a new front door or paint it a fresh, complementary color.
- [ ] Create an inviting outdoor space by adding new seating, side tables and outdoor lanterns.
- [ ] Replace all fixtures to match the style your home.
- [ ] Spray for any bugs such as spiders or wasps. Make sure all areas are clear of pests.

On The Market
TIME TO SELL YOUR HOME

The June's Team

LISTING PLAN OF ACTION

OUR OBJECTIVES ARE THE FOLLOWING:

1. <u>Maximize Buyer Exposure:</u> Our goal is to attract numerous qualified buyers to view your home, continuing diligently until the right offer is secured.
2. <u>Regular Progress Updates:</u> We commit to keeping you informed with weekly updates, sharing the outcomes of our marketing efforts and buyer feedback.
3. <u>Optimize Your Sale:</u> Our expertise is in negotiating not just a favorable sale price but also the best terms, ensuring you get the maximum value from your transaction.
4. <u>Personalized Support:</u> We also aim to provide tailored advice and support throughout the selling process, addressing any concerns and making the experience as seamless as possible for you.

AN OVERVIEW OF THE STEPS WE TAKE TO SELL A HOME:

Initial Consultation: We start with a meeting to understand your specific needs, timeline, and any unique aspects of your home. This helps us tailor our approach to your situation.

Market Analysis and Pricing: We conduct a comprehensive market analysis to determine a competitive yet profitable listing price for your home. This includes reviewing comparable sales and current market trends.

Home Preparation: Our team advises on staging and necessary repairs or improvements to enhance your home's appeal. We focus on maximizing its strengths and addressing any potential drawbacks.

Professional Photography: High-quality photos are essential. We arrange for professional photographers to capture your home in its best light, ensuring the visuals attract potential buyers.

Listing and Marketing: Your home is listed on relevant platforms. We implement a strategic marketing plan, which includes digital marketing, social media promotion, and possibly open houses, to maximize exposure.

Handling Showings: We coordinate and manage home showings, offering flexibility to accommodate potential buyers' schedules while respecting your privacy and convenience.

Offer and Negotiation: Once offers are received, we review them with you and handle negotiations. Our goal is to achieve the best possible price and terms for you.

Transaction Management: After accepting an offer, we manage the entire transaction process. This includes coordinating with inspectors, appraisers, and closing agents, ensuring all necessary paperwork is complete and deadlines are met.

Closing: We guide you through the closing process, ensuring you understand all aspects of the final paperwork. Our team is there to answer any questions and make sure everything proceeds smoothly.

Post-Sale Support: Even after the sale, we remain available to assist with any post-closing needs or questions you might have.

LISTING PHOTOS

After all that prep work, you want your listing photos to showcase your home in its best light. Capturing a home's attributes can influence a property's time on the market and final sale price. We will arrange to have the photos taken by a professional real estate photographer.

Preparing for listing photos is crucial, as these images will make the first impression on potential buyers. Here are some quick tips for the best listing photos.

- Declutter: Remove excess items and personal belongings for a clean, spacious look.
- Deep Clean: Ensure the home is spotless, including windows, for a pristine appearance.
- Stage Strategically: Arrange furniture to showcase each room's purpose and space.
- Neutralize Decor: Opt for neutral colors and remove personal items like family photos.
- Enhance Lighting: Open curtains and blinds and turn on all lights to brighten the space.
- Highlight Key Features: Make sure unique aspects of the home are visible and well-presented.
- Tidy Exteriors: Clean up the yard, porch, and driveway for an inviting first impression.
- Add Greenery: A few well-placed plants can add life and color to the rooms.

PRICING YOUR HOME

In today's market, buyers are well-informed and specific about what they want. They come prepared with knowledge about the neighborhoods they're interested in, the features they desire in a home, and a clear idea of what they're willing to pay. Remember, their goal isn't necessarily to meet your asking price, but to pay a price that reflects what they perceive as your home's true value.

At June's Team, we understand the pitfalls of overpricing. Statistically, homes attract the most buyer interest in the first two weeks after listing. Setting the price too high during this crucial period can result in lost momentum and interest.

The true value of a home, ultimately, is what a buyer is ready to pay for it. To guide you in setting the right price, we'll analyze recently listed and sold properties in your area, focusing on homes that match yours in style and location. Furthermore, we provide an Estimated Market Value report, derived from a thorough review of comparable sales over the past six months. This approach ensures that your home is priced not just competitively, but also realistically, aligning with current market trends and buyer expectations

HERE'S HOW WE WILL SET THE RIGHT PRICE FOR YOUR HOME:

1 In-Depth Market Analysis: We conduct thorough research on current market trends, specifically focusing on properties similar to yours in terms of size, condition, and location. This helps us gain a clear understanding of what buyers are willing to pay in your area.

2 Strategic Initial Pricing: Our experience shows that homes priced correctly from the outset tend to sell faster and at a better price. We help you find that sweet spot for your listing price, balancing market appeal with the true value of your home.

3 Utilizing Appraisals and CMAs: We recommend professional appraisals and provide Comparative Market Analysis (CMAs) to give you an objective view of your home's value. These tools are crucial in understanding how your home compares to others in the area.

4 Accounting for Unique Features: Your home is unique, and we recognize that. We'll help you adjust your price based on special features, upgrades, or areas that might need improvement, ensuring these factors are accurately reflected in the valuation.

5 Flexible Pricing Strategy: The market can be unpredictable, and buyer responses are a great indicator of your pricing strategy's effectiveness. We stay alert and ready to adjust your pricing if necessary, ensuring your home remains competitive in the market.

With June's Team, you're not just setting a price; you're positioning your home for the best possible outcome in the Northern Colorado real estate market.

MARKETING

YOUR FIRST SHOWING IS ONLINE
Your home will get the exposure it deserves. Our marketing systems maximize your property's exposure to buyers. Neighborhood tracking tools and automated buyer calling systems allow us to reach active buyers who want to know about your listing. According to the National Association of Realtors, buyers that started their search on the internet went from 8% to over 90% in recent years. Nowadays, your first showing is on the internet. That is why having a company and agent with an internet-focused marketing system is key. Pricing has to be considered, so you will be in more than one price bracket at a time. Buyers search in price brackets, therefore it is better to be priced at $500k than $499k. This way, you will appear in searches for homes priced from $450k to $500k, and in searches for homes priced from $500k to $550k.

YARD SIGNS
We will put a sign in your yard right away. It will say "coming soon" if we place it before your listing is active. Many of the calls we get from yard signs turn into appointments with buyers! We never miss an opportunity for a showing with a team approach!

MARKETING A LUXURY HOME
Across Northern Colorado, homes priced above $550,000 are marketed as luxury or upper-bracket properties. When selling a luxury home, it is critical that sellers know what to expect. Upper-bracket properties require specific marketing strategies and often behave differently on the market than homes at lower price points. Because there are fewer buyers qualified to purchase your property, it may take longer to sell. That's why it is key to work with a Realtor who is familiar with your area and well-versed in selling luxury properties.

Our Targeted Marketing Plan
FOR YOUR HOME

AT JUNE'S TEAM, WE'VE DEVELOPED A STRATEGIC APPROACH TO ENSURE YOUR HOME RECEIVES MAXIMUM EXPOSURE AND ATTRACTS SERIOUS BUYERS. HERE'S HOW WE'LL MARKET YOUR PROPERTY:

1. Comprehensive Online Listings:
   - MLS (Multiple Listing Service): Your home will be listed on the MLS, ensuring visibility to real estate professionals and buyers nationwide.
   - Top Real Estate Websites: We'll feature your home on all major real estate platforms like Zillow, Realtor.com, Trulia, and Redfin.
   - June's Team Website: A dedicated listing on our website, complete with a detailed description, and professional photos.

2. Digital Marketing Campaign:
   - Social Media Advertising: Targeted posts on Facebook, Instagram, and LinkedIn to reach potential buyers. Facebook Marketplace and Nextdoor are also utilized spaces to advertise your home.
   - Google Ads: Campaigns to capture the interest of buyers searching for homes in Northern Colorado.
   - Email Marketing: A targeted email blast to our curated list of potential buyers and local real estate agents.

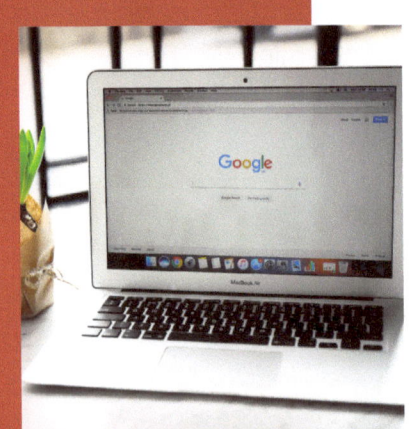

3. Professional Photography and Videos:
   - High-Quality Photography: Professional photos to showcase your home's best features.
   - Different styles of videos will be taken of your home to utilize the reels marketing on Facebook and Instagram.

4. Print Marketing Materials:
   - Brochures and Flyers: Professionally designed brochures and flyers to be distributed at open houses and local businesses.
   - Local Newspapers and Magazines: Ad placements in local newspapers and real estate magazines.

5. Open Houses and Private Showings:
   - Public Open Houses: Regularly scheduled open houses to welcome potential buyers. These are also advertised on social media.
   - Broker Open Houses: Exclusive viewings for local real estate agents to increase industry buzz.
   - Private Showings: Personalized tours for interested buyers, arranged to fit their schedules.

6. Community Engagement and Networking:
   - Local Community Boards & Events: Posting about your listing on community bulletin boards and online community forums. June is very active in the community and regularly attends local networking events.
   - Real Estate Networking Events: Promoting your home at industry events and meetups.

7. Feedback and Market Response Analysis:
   - We'll gather feedback from showings and open houses and analyze market responses, adjusting our strategy as needed to ensure your home stays competitive.

Our goal is to not just list your home but to actively market it, ensuring it reaches the right audience and sells for the best price. Trust in June's Team to bring our full suite of marketing tools and expertise to the table.

MARKETING TO FIRST TIME HOME BUYERS

In the Northern Colorado market, "starter homes" are typically valued at $400,000 or below (Business Insider 2023). First-time home buyers care more about how space is used, rather than square footage. Do not underestimate the power of staging your home to show how every inch of space can be maximized. Any upgrades that make the home more modern and move-in ready can also give your home an advantage.

SELLER DISCLOSURES

Sellers in Colorado are required to make disclosures to buyers in connection with the sale. Sellers must disclose all significant, adverse material facts about the property. This obligation includes the duty to disclose all defects with the property that affect it's value, it's useful life, or the health and safety of its occupants. Making a complete disclosure is the best way for you to avoid liability from the sale of your home. In Colorado, you must satisfy the disclosure requirement by completing a Seller Property Disclosure Form providing information to the best of you knowledge. In addition, there are other disclosure forms based on the area and age of the home. Don't worry, we will help guide you through this disclosure process.

WHAT IS A HOME WARRANTY AND SHOULD YOU CONSIDER IT?

Sellers can protect the equity investment in their home with a home warranty company. The home warranty can help protect the seller's budget from costly surprise repairs and replacement of the home's covered major mechanical system components and appliances. Adding a home warranty during the listing period may help reduce your "out-of-pocket" expenses from a covered breakdown.

Seller Insight: Tankless water heaters are popular with buyers.

YOUR NEXT HOME

When your projects are complete and your listing is ready to go, it is time to start thinking about purchasing your next home. Figure out your budget early on in this process. Talk to a lender about getting pre-approved for a mortgage so you can determine your price range and have the upper hand over buyers who are not pre-approved. We are happy to give you recommendations for great mortgage professionals.

Then, we will work together to:
- See how your criteria and budget match up to today's inventory of homes.
- Rank your criteria and budget accordingly.
- Take time to tour homes and assess their pros and cons.

GOING "LIVE"

While your home is listed we will monitor your competition in regard to price, and strategize with you to make any adjustments on price, condition, and marketing. We will contact you weekly to review showings and feedback, and will answer any questions that you may have regarding your listing, the market, and the marketing of your home.

We will let you know any time we receive an inquiry on your home. This helps us gauge interest, based on our ability to get the client into your house. If we are getting inquiries but no showings, then there is an issue with perceived value.

When we receive an offer and proceed to closing:

We will maintain communication with all parties throughout the process, and let you know what to expect every step of the way. We will also be your contact from executed contract to closing.

We negotiate contracts, the inspection, appraisal issues, and any additional addendas that are necessary. We will assist throughout the process until your home is sold, and we will sit with you at the closing table.

SHOWING YOUR HOME

You have spruced up your home, decided on a price and we have worked on a marketing strategy. It is time to show it off!

Home showings: What to expect

Once your home is listed, showings can happen quickly. Realtors request a viewing of your home on behalf of their buyers. With your permission, these potential buyers spend 30-60 minutes in your home with their agents, often comparing it to other homes.

During a seller's market, there can be multiple showings of your home in the first 48 hours, so be prepared to be busy and not in your home during the first few days. When you work with June's Team, all showings are set up through a paid system called Showing Time and you will receive a request to have your property shown via text, email, or a phone call, whichever you selected during your listing appointment. You simply need to reply to the requests with a Y (okay to show my home) or a N (Sorry, not a good time) response! It is that easy!

SHOWING TIPS

It is critical that your home is show-ready at all times. When your home is being shown, please do the following:

- Keep all lights on
- Make sure the home is clean, beds are made, and everything is picked up
- Keep all drapes and shutters open
- Keep all interior doors unlocked
- Leave soft music playing
- Take a short excursion with your children and pets
- Let your buyer be at ease and not rushed

TIPS FOR HOLDING AN OPEN HOUSE

- We will bring snacks and drinks.
- Alert the neighbors, so they can anticipate traffic or parking near their homes.
- Set up a table and chairs with festive outdoor place settings to show that your home's entertaining space extends beyond its walls.
- In addition to an official listing flyer, you can create a short overview of local highlights such as parks and shopping areas.

DON'T BE AFRAID OF BUYER FEEDBACK

If your home is not selling, you will want to know why. At June's Team, we provide sellers with an exclusive weekly update. During this update, we will share how many showings, marketing, and open houses we have held and provide feedback directly from agents who have viewed your home.

HOW LONG WILL IT TAKE TO SELL YOUR HOME?

We can talk about how long homes in your area are typically on the market before selling. While this is not a hard and fast predictor, it can help set expectations for timing. The market is variable and can change quickly, but with our experience, we will do our best to anticipate what is coming next.

COSTLY EMOTIONAL MISTAKES TO AVOID

Insider Tip #1

The first step to emotionally detaching from your home is recognizing that your home is not perfect. You will be showing off your home's best features to draw in a higher offer, but buyers may focus on the property's flaws to get a better deal. Remember this isn't a personal attack - you are just on opposite sides of a business transaction.

Insider Tip #2

To appeal to most buyers, it is critical that your home be free of clutter and staged to show off its best features. Additionally, your home should be spotless any time you leave the house so you can accept last-minute showings without rushing home to wash the dishes or make the bed. If your home has been on the market a while, it's common to become apathetic to showings. However, by showing off your home's best assets every time you have a showing request, you will be showing each buyer that your home is worth its listing price.

Insider Tip #3

While you may be curious about potential buyers, you should not remain in your home during showings or open houses. Buyers need to be able to freely look at each room of the home and share feedback with their family, friends, and agent. By remaining in your home, you could stifle the buyer's interest.

Insider Tip #4

If you get an offer within the first few days on the market, you may believe you have priced your home too low. While this is an understandable reaction, the reality is that buyers are much more eager to look at (and make offers on) homes that have just entered the market. It is proven that homes receive the most interest - both in terms of showings and offers - in the first two weeks after they are listed on the MLS.
On the other hand, homes that remain on the market for extended periods of time are often less appealing to buyers, who may believe that something is wrong with them. If you get an early offer on a house, be sure not to take it the wrong way. Together we can determine what the offer means and if you should hold out for more competing offers or accept this fast path to the closing table.

The path to
CLOSING

GUIDING YOU THROUGH THE OFFER PROCESS

Understanding Contingencies:
Buyers may include contingencies in their offer, like needing to sell their current home or pending satisfactory inspection reports. We'll carefully review these with you to evaluate their impact and decide whether to accept contingent offers, considering both the time and financial aspects involved.

Navigating Negotiations:
If an offer doesn't fully meet your expectations but shows potential, we can strategize a counteroffer. This step is crucial in ensuring your interests are well-represented.

Handling Multiple Offers:
Receiving multiple offers is an excellent position as a seller. It puts you in control and can lead to a more favorable sale. However, the best offer isn't always the highest bid. Factors like closing costs, timelines, and buyer financing play significant roles. We'll analyze each offer's details to help you understand and choose the one that truly aligns with your goals.

Accepting an Offer:
Once you accept an offer, congratulations are in order! From here, we move forward with a series of steps, typically involving a twelve-stage process (explained in the coming pages), leading up to the closing. Each selling experience is unique, so our approach will be personalized to your situation, ensuring a smooth journey to the final transaction.

From Accepting an Offer TO THE CLOSING TABLE

1 Loan Application: The buyer initiates the process by applying for a mortgage loan to finance the purchase of the home.

2 Title Commitment: A title company is engaged to issue a title commitment, ensuring the property title is clear of any liens or claims and ready for transfer.

3 Due Diligence: The buyer conducts due diligence, researching the property's history, zoning, and any other pertinent details that might affect their decision to purchase. An Improvement Location Certificate is used to estimate property lines.

4 Home Inspection: A professional home inspector assesses the property for any structural, electrical, or plumbing issues or any other potential concerns.

5 Appraisal: The lender orders an appraisal of the property to confirm its market value meets or exceeds the loan amount.

6 Homeowner's Insurance: The buyer obtains homeowner's insurance, a requirement for mortgage approval, to protect against future property damage or liability.

7 Re-Inspections if Necessary: If the initial inspection uncovers issues, re-inspections may be necessary post-repairs to ensure all problems are resolved.

8 Loan Approval: The lender finalizes the loan approval, confirming the buyer's financing is secure and the purchase can proceed.

9 Schedule Closing Time and Place: Both parties agree on a date, time, and location for the closing meeting, where the transfer of ownership will be finalized.

10 Walk-Through: Just before closing, the buyer does a final walk-through of the property to ensure its condition hasn't changed and agreed-upon repairs have been completed.

11 Update Your Address & Transfer Utilities: The seller updates their address for future correspondence and initiates the transfer of utilities to the buyer.

12 Closing Time: It's Here! At the closing meeting, both parties sign all necessary documents, the seller receives the payment, and the buyer officially becomes the new homeowner.

QUICK TIPS FOR PASSING AN INSPECTION

1. Fix Minor Repairs: Address small issues like leaky faucets, loose doorknobs, or missing tiles before the inspection.

2. Check Electrical Systems: Make sure all outlets, switches, and fixtures work. Replace any burnt-out light bulbs to avoid a negative report on the electrical system.

3. Ensure Plumbing Works Properly: Test all faucets and toilets for leaks or running water. Clean out under-sink areas to provide easy access for the inspector.

4. Inspect the HVAC System: Change filters and have the HVAC system serviced if it hasn't been done recently. Ensure the system is functioning properly.

5. Clear Access to Key Areas: Ensure that areas like the furnace, water heater, electrical panel, and attic entrance are easily accessible.

6. Clean and Declutter: A clean home gives a good impression. Make sure the house is tidy, with no clutter obstructing critical areas or systems.

7. Check Smoke and Carbon Monoxide Detectors: Ensure they are in working order and have fresh batteries.

8. Examine the Roof: Look for missing or damaged shingles and clean the gutters.

9. Address Exterior Issues: Secure loose siding or trim, make sure downspouts are draining away from the foundation, and check for any standing water.

10. Prepare Documentation: Have receipts or documentation ready for any major repairs or maintenance work done on the home.

THE APPRAISAL

What does an appraiser do?

In short, an appraiser determines the current value of a property. They do this by performing a walk-through of the property making note of amenities that add or detract value. They will also note health and safety code violations and other areas of concern. Appraisers will utilize comparable home data (often referred to as "comps") of nearby recent sales of same-style homes to help determine a home's value.

What does an appraiser do?

Appraisers are independent contractors hired by the lender and typically billed to the buyer. While they are on your property, it is essential to allow them one to two hours to complete the inspection without interruption.

What happens if the home appraises?

Yay! Your property was appraised at the sales price! All systems are go and you are on your way to the closing table. Now the buyer's lender, providing the buyer's financing is otherwise in order, will approve the home mortgage loan and it will be submitted to the title company to prepare the documents for closing. It will go back through underwriting to be reviewed and the final loan conditions will be cleared.

What happens if the home does not appraise?

If a home appraises for less than the sale price, it can complicate the transaction, particularly if the buyer is financing the purchase with a mortgage. The lender will only fund up to the appraised value, which may lead to renegotiations between the buyer and seller, often resulting in a lower sale price. Alternatively, the buyer might cover the difference or some of the difference out-of-pocket. If an agreement can't be reached, the seller might dispute the appraisal or the deal could fall through, prompting the seller to seek other buyers. The resolution depends largely on the flexibility of both parties and the contract terms. FHA appraisals stick with a property for 6 months.

THE CLOSING

The closing process finalizes the sale of your home and makes everything official. Also known as settlement, the closing is when you get paid and the buyer receives the deed and keys to your home.

SELLERS COMMONLY PAY THE FOLLOWING AT CLOSING:

- Mortgage balance and prepayment penalties, if applicable
- Other claims against your property, such as property taxes
- Unpaid special assessments on your property
- Document stamps (or taxes) on the deed
- Real estate commission
- Legal fees or title insurance premium

AFTER THE CLOSING, MAKE SURE YOU KEEP THE FOLLOWING FOR TAX PURPOSES:

- Copies of all closing documents
- All home improvement receipts on the home you sold

WHAT TO BRING TO CLOSING:

- House keys
- Mailbox key
- Garage door opener(s)
- Your valid photo ID

THE CLOSING APPOINTMENT

The closing agent will look over the purchase contract and identify what payments are owed and by whom; prepare documents for the closing; conduct the closing; make sure all taxes, title searches, real estate commissions, and other closing costs are paid; ensure that the buyer's title is recorded; and ensure that you receive any money due to you.

MORE INSIGHTS:

- You will be contacted by the closing agent.
- Ask the closer about their online security procedures to prevent cyber-fraud.
- Verify or update your personal information.
- We will set up your closing date and time.
- Provide instructions for seller proceeds.
- Attend closing to sign all paperwork and turn over the keys.
- The closing process usually takes about an hour.

Congratulations!
YOU'VE SOLD YOUR HOME

As you reach the final pages of this guide, you stand at an important crossroads in your journey to sell your home. The decision of whom to trust with this significant step is crucial. By choosing June's Team, you're not just selecting a real estate service; you're partnering with a dedicated team committed to turning your selling goals into reality. We understand the complexities and nuances of the Northern Colorado market and promise to navigate each step with the utmost care and professionalism. When you're ready to take this leap, know that we are here, equipped with the expertise, dedication, and personalized approach to ensure your selling experience is not just successful, but also rewarding. We look forward to the opportunity to celebrate the successful sale of your home with you and to being an integral part of your journey to new beginnings.

What's Next? Decide to work together. Let's make it official!

Answering all your
QUESTIONS

SELLER FAQ'S

Q. I have a friend in the business, shouldn't I use them?

A. I can certainly appreciate this and in this, and in this market almost everyone does. Do you absolutely have to sell this home, or are you looking to do a friend a favor?

As the seller, you need to consider this a business decision and ask yourself:
- Which agent will I financially benefit from hiring?
- If something goes awry, would I want it to impact that friendship?
- Can I tell my friend how I truly feel when a situation arises, or will it impact my decision?
- Do I want my friend to know my personal assets and what goes along with it?
- Can I fire my friend? (You can fire us if you are not 100% satisfied with our service.)

Q. Why do some agents claim they can get me more money?

A. There are several possible answers:
1. An agent that will list your property overpriced assumes they can take the listing now, then they will start beating you up on the price week after week because your property isn't selling.
2. They are telling you whatever you want to hear, to take your listing because they know that by having a listing, potential buyers will call them. Some agents will do this so they can switch the buyers to other, better-priced, properties where they will get paid a full commission.
3. They simply aren't paying attention to the market. Is this the type of agent you want working for you?

Q. How important is it to be familiar or comfortable with the company you hire?

A. Choosing a real estate team you're comfortable and familiar with is crucial. It's about more than just transactions; it's a partnership for a major life decision. A trusted realtor ensures ease of communication, personalized service, and a less stressful experience. Comfort with your real estate team fosters trust, which is essential for effectively navigating the complexities of buying or selling a home. We would never recommend that you work with someone you're uncomfortable with.

SELLER FAQ'S

Q. Why wouldn't we save the commission by selling it ourselves?

A. Opting to sell your home on your own can seem appealing at first, primarily for the potential savings on commission. However, it's important to consider the broader picture. Statistics show that only a small percentage of For Sale By Owner (FSBO) homes successfully sell without professional assistance. The reality is, that navigating the complexities of a home sale – from marketing and negotiation to legal compliance – can be a daunting task. Additionally, buyers aware of an FSBO situation often expect a lower price, anticipating that they should share in the commission savings. This can lead to a situation where, instead of saving on commission, you might end up with a lower selling price. Professional representation by a real estate agent like June's Team not only increases your chances of a successful sale but also ensures that your interests are expertly represented, potentially resulting in better financial outcomes and a smoother process overall.

Q. Should we list high? We can always come down in price later.

A. It's a common thought to start with a higher listing price to give room for negotiation. However, this strategy can have some unintended consequences. A key point to consider is the market's perception. Homes priced above market value tend to deter potential buyers, especially those who are well-informed and working within a specific budget. These buyers are likely to overlook a property that appears overpriced, potentially reducing the pool of interested parties. What we aim for is to create a scenario where your home attracts considerable interest, ideally leading to competitive offers. This is often achieved through accurate pricing that reflects the current market, drawing in serious buyers and setting the stage for effective negotiations. Our goal at June's Team is to price your home in a way that maximizes both interest and value, ensuring you receive the best possible outcome from the sale.

Q. How long should we think it over?

A: It's essential to take the time you need to make a confident decision. Let's discuss any concerns or questions you have during our meeting. At June's Team, we're committed to helping you make a well-informed choice that aligns with your goals, and we're here to provide guidance and support throughout your decision-making process.

SELLER FAQ'S

Q. Is it important to have an agent who sells a lot of homes in a specific area?

A. Absolutely. Choosing an agent with extensive experience and a broad reach in the market, like myself, is advantageous. June's Team handles properties across the area, which means that when you list with me, your home gains exposure to a wide pool of potential buyers, not just locally, but nationally. This level of marketing exposure is essential in finding the right buyer for your home and ensuring a successful sale.

Q. Will you cut your commission, as other agents have offered to do?

A. I understand why the idea of a reduced commission can be appealing. However, it's important to consider the value you receive in exchange for that commission. In real estate, the strength and negotiation skills of your agent are crucial. An agent confident in their value tends to be more effective in defending your home's price and ensuring you get the best possible outcome. Discounted services might save you in upfront costs, but they often don't deliver the same level of dedication and results, which can be critical in a successful and profitable home sale. At June's Team, we're committed to providing top-tier service that justifies our commission through the results we achieve for you.

Q. How long should we list for?

A. In the current market, where homes may take longer to sell, it's crucial to price your home competitively from the start. If we don't see the desired response within the first 30 days, we should be prepared to adjust our strategy. With aggressive initial pricing and a flexible approach to market feedback, our goal would be to successfully sell your home within 120 days. This proactive and responsive plan is key to navigating today's market effectively.

Q. What sets your approach to selling homes apart from other agents?

A. Our approach at June's Team is centered around a personalized and proactive strategy. We don't just list your home; we actively market it. This includes using a mix of traditional and innovative marketing techniques, from high-quality photography and videography to targeted digital advertising and community networking. We also emphasize transparent and frequent communication with you, ensuring you're informed and involved at every step. Our deep understanding of the Northern Colorado market, combined with our commitment to your individual needs, allows us to provide a service that's not just effective, but also tailored to your unique selling journey.

Choosing to work with June's Team means you're not just getting exceptional real estate services; you're stepping into a seamless and stress-free experience. Our comprehensive approach connects all aspects of your transaction, from mortgages and title services to insurance, warranties, and even relocation assistance. It's like having a one-stop solution for all your real estate needs. We're excited to collaborate with you to create a personalized plan that not only sells your home but does so at the best possible value. Let's discuss when you're ready to start this journey, and we'll take care of the rest, ensuring a swift and satisfying sale.

How can we help?

June Lemmings

970-573-5791 Office
970-388-3692 Cell
www.junelemmings.com
june@junesteam.com